A ROUTINE FOR LIFE

ACTIVITY WORKBOOK

12 Lessons Designed to Help Children
Grow Spiritually and Add Value to
Society. (Children ages 6-14)

MARIAN E. AMOA

WESTBOW
PRESS®
A DIVISION OF THOMAS NELSON
& ZONDERVAN

WestBow Press books may be ordered through booksellers or by contacting:

WestBow Press
A Division of Thomas Nelson & Zondervan
1663 Liberty Drive
Bloomington, IN 47403
www.westbowpress.com
844-714-3454

ISBN: 978-1-6642-4521-1 (sc)
ISBN: 978-1-6642-4520-4 (e)

Print information available on the last page.

WestBow Press rev. date: 12/28/2021

Date

This Book Belongs To

_____

CONTENTS

INTRODUCTION

In every crisis, there is an opportunity. Such was the coronavirus (Covid-19) pandemic of 2020. If I were to select a Bible verse that describes this pandemic, it will be Romans 8:28 NLT – "And we know that God causes everything to work together for the good of those who love God and are called according to his purpose for them." So, while we do not understand it all, we know that God is in control, and even in this painful "storm," God has been in control. It was during this period that I developed a curriculum – A Routine for Life: Twelve Lessons Designed to Help Children Grow Spiritually and Add Value to Society. This activity workbook is a companion to the curriculum.

You will find in this activity book materials that reinforce learnings from the curriculum. The curriculum focuses on creating a routine based on five main activities – Read your Bible, Pray, Be Helpful, Be Kind, Be Thankful. Included in this workbook are –

Student review & practice sheet – enables you to review what you learned.

Life Giver Challenge– helps you find ways to practice what you learned.

Word searches – help you remember and recognize the Bible passage/text and improves your problem-solving abilities.

Mazes – help you improve your fine motor and visual skills, enhance your problem-solving skills and boost your confidence.

Crossword puzzles – enhance your problem-solving abilities, help you learn patience, and perseverance.

Match the verse activity – encourages you to search the Bible for key verses.

Coloring pages –improve your fine motor skills, encourages the brain to focus, and nurtures creativity. It is a low-cost way to relax.

Additional Resources - You can access additional resources on www.geedeecreative.com.

You can watch the short video clips on the five topics—Read your Bible, Pray, Be Helpful, Be Kind, and Be Thankful—via YouTube at GeeDee Creative.

Dear Friend,

I am happy that you picked this activity workbook. Maybe for you, it is part of your Children's Church curriculum or your home Bible study or even a fun club. Or perhaps, you picked it up out of curiosity.

No matter how you found yourself with this copy, I am excited you have it. It is my desire that you find some nuggets that you can apply to your everyday day life. I pray that these activities will enhance your life's journey and every aspect of it – your life at home, at church, at school, at work, at the gym, you name it.

I believe the curriculum, alongside the activities in this workbook will add value to your life and help you grow in the Lord, and it will help you become relevant in every sphere of your life.

Read and reflect on the scriptures, ask questions about what you do not understand, and write down your reflections. Practice what you learn. Enjoy the coloring pages and be as creative as you can. Challenge yourself with the word puzzles and the mazes, and do not forget the life giver challenges for each lesson.

Working on this activity workbook has been an exciting experience for me. I hope you will enjoy it as much as I did when I was putting it together. Enjoy!

> *"For this very reason, make every effort to add to your faith goodness; and to goodness, knowledge; and to knowledge, self-control; and to self-control, perseverance; and to perseverance, godliness; and to godliness, mutual affection; and to mutual affection, love. For if you possess these qualities in increasing measure, they will keep you from being ineffective and unproductive in your knowledge of our Lord Jesus Christ." (2 Peter 1:5-8 NIV)*

A ROUTINE FOR LIFE

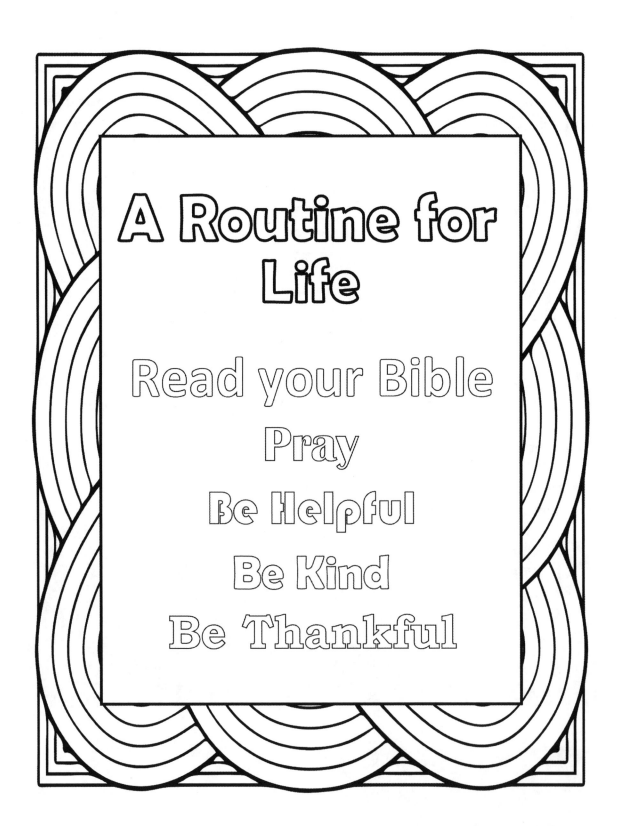

LESSON ONE

Introduction to Routine
Student Review and Practice Sheet

What is Routine?

Routine is doing something over and over again till it becomes a part of you, till it becomes a habit.

Our Routine

(1) Read your Bible
(2) Pray
(3) Be kind
(4) Be helpful
(5) Be thankful

Scriptures: Mark 1:35, Luke 5:16, Daniel 6:10, 1 Sam 1:3, Psalm 55:17.

Memory verse: Daniel 6:10b (NLT): "He prayed three times a day, just as he had always done, giving thanks to his God."

Life-Giver challenge: Create your routine by adding to our routine list. Keep notes or check marks on what you do each day.

What I learned today:

_____

_____

_____

_____

_____

_____

_____

_____

_____

What I plan to do:

_____

_____

_____

_____

_____

_____

_____

_____

_____

A Routine for Life Poster

LESSON ONE

Daniel 6:10 NLT

"But when Daniel learned that the law had been signed, he went home and knelt down as usual in his upstairs room, with its windows open toward Jerusalem. He prayed three times a day, just as he had always done, giving thanks to his God." Daniel 6:10 NLT

Psalm 55:17 NKJV

"Evening and morning and at noon I will pray, and cry aloud, And He shall hear my voice."

Psalm 55:17 NKJV

Maze 1 – Find your way out of the maze to your next activity.

Crossword Puzzle 1 – Read the Scriptures to help you solve the puzzle.

Scriptures – Mark 1:35, Luke 5:16, Daniel 6:10, Psalm 55:17, 1 Samuel 1:3a

Across

4. Every year he went to this _____ to offer sacrifices.
5. He gave _____ to God just as he had always done.
6. He prayed three times a day just as he had always done.
7. Jesus often withdrew to a lonely place and _____.

Down

1. This man went to his city every year to offer sacrifices.
2. Very early in the morning he prayed.
3. _____ is doing something over and over again till it becomes a habit.
6. He prayed evening, morning and at noon.

Introduction to Routine
(ages 6 – 10)

Word List

1.Read   2.Bible   3.Pray   4.Kind   5.Help   6.Thankful   7.Habit   8.Usual
9.Often   10.Jesus   11.God   12.Three   13.Times   14.Routine   15.Voice

---

```
W U X O J F U W F B Z U B A C J
M T Q K X R R M F P O B Q H I B
U X C R A T Z Q P H R S L Y C G
Y T S D K R A P A F E D K J U Q
T G Y S X Z D O Y M K L I T U Z
V F G T K Y Q F I V I M P W R B
F X X O Q J J T H R E E F A V L
M F E H V V R E A D H B K V R V
X A T U Y K O N S Z G L I D U O
T H A N K F U L K U T O N B B I
B V T G A W T S K O S Y D H L C
Z U T N F Q I V A A R P R A Y E
F T A L C Z N E R X B F U B L R
L D J N O U E L D H I S C I U A
E W T U I T J C W H U U I T E B
R A M N S O C I K W D G F P O Y
```

Introduction to Routine
(ages 10 – 14)

Word List

1.Read   2.Bible   3.Pray   4.Kind   5.Help   6.Thankful   7.Always
8.Daniel   9.Jesus   10.Habit   11.Voice   12.Weekly   13.Family   14.Worship
15.Usual   16.Morning   17.Evening   18.Routine   19.Elkanah   20.God

```
C G A D A H U R M E I I D P R Z
W O R S H I P C W L S A X P A E
G D A N I E L D U K R Z R T K L
J H Z D H V V F D U V C Y N L K
Y I P G W E K P L E H H B W X W
X C S V L N L X X T I S V H T Y
E U Q N A I G P S V F B C S F U
E Y G H C N A X H X G W S K A D
C N T N I G F H A X K P V N M W
Z M Q N O D C R A L W A Y S I E
W A R Z B H Z Q R B I V V N L E
K O N C L U K N L F I I O B Y K
M Z B F H K S F R O U T I N E L
I L G P J I I U E E V B C O A Y
S K C E L K A N A H V J E S U S
N W N R B W F I D L L O P R A Y
```

LESSON TWO

Daniel's Routine
Student Review and Practice Sheet

What is Routine? Routine is doing something over and over again till it becomes a part of you, till it becomes a habit.

Our Routine

(1) Read your Bible
(2) Pray
(3) Be kind
(4) Be helpful
(5) Be thankful

Read: Daniel chapter 6.

Memory verse: Daniel 6:10b (NLT): "He prayed three times a day, just as he had always done, giving thanks to his God."

Life-Giver challenge: Write down three things you learned about Daniel. Keep track of your routine. Keep notes or check marks on what you do each day.

What I learned today:

_____

_____

_____

_____

_____

_____

_____

_____

_____

_____

What I plan to do:

_____

_____

_____

_____

_____

_____

_____

_____

_____

_____

Daniel prayed three times a day (Daniel 6:10) Version 1

Daniel prayed three times a day (Daniel 6:10) Version 2

Maze 2 - Find your way out of the maze to your next activity.

Crossword Puzzle 2 – Read the Scriptures to help you solve the puzzle.

Scripture – Daniel 6 (NLT)

Across

4. King_____ appointed 120 satraps to rule throughout the kingdom.
6. Daniel said that God sent an angel to shut the _____ of the lions.
8. He prayed three times a day and he gave thanks to God as he always did.
9. When Daniel learned that the decree had been published, he went home, to his upstairs room where the windows opened toward _____.

Down

1. Daniel distinguished himself and had exceptional _____.
2. The king said to Daniel that may the God he serves _____ him.
3. Anyone who _____to any god or human being during the next thirty days will be thrown into the lions' den.
5. The administrators and the satraps tried to find grounds for _____ against Daniel in his conduct of government affairs.
7. King Darius put the_____ in writing.

LESSON TWO

Daniel's Routine
(ages 6 – 10)

Word List

1.Law   2.Daniel   3.Three   4.Times   5.Usual   6.Room
7.Home   8.Routine   9.Lion   10.Den   11.Kind
12.Help   13.Thankful   14.Pray   15.Read

```
T Y C N U R O T Y D T Y M F P A
F I W U P O V B I W Z A C H S H
J Q P L J Q D N E N O A K Q X C
V S L U P N F E J C E D A F X R
N Q Q L I O N K L P V Q E Q P V
R H B K N I K L L U E I R N C C
A N L I T H A N K F U L J L Q N
Z Y K U A E H G U F O U E U O B
B R O S O T D N S F Z C I H J P
I R O O M E W H U D E D D E N I
C E D K H Y E N A Y T W E L J H
O A Y D A N I E L M U R Q P A U
S D M R A T Z H S U H R E Y A W
S N P B P K T Y N T I M E S H H
P Q O L C T A V Q W O K G N L S
D O D W S M M O X H B I I R D F
```

Daniel's Routine
(ages 10 – 14)

Word List

1.Daniel 2.Faithful 3.Decree 4.Upstairs 5.Room 6.Home 7.Routine
8.Thankful 9.Helpful 10.Kind 11.Pray 12.Bible 13.Lion
14.Usual 15.Habit 16.Three 17.Times 18.King 19.God 20.Learned

```
M F K K E U X E H Z Y G G Q M M
A E Q S W G E O K V C K E H I H
D U U K B W T X T B W K P T B Z
G E R T I M E S H M C I H B L C
S G C H B N G F A I T H F U L B
V A I R L S D N N A A Q Q S L M
T T H E E O Z H K F C C R U E E
I S O E J E Z B F X F I W A F C
N Q M R C A N S U C A T A L I Q
F L E A R N E D L T A J E P S C
D W P E O B W N S H Z I T L D V
U K J Z U D G P M B N M T Y T N
A J E W T N U O S A M I I N Y Q
M E C S I J O N D J B O O A V O
S O Z K N R Q Q F A O I R F W B
F N G E E J I P H E L P F U L U
```

LESSON THREE

Read Your Bible
Student Review and Practice Sheet

What is Routine? Routine is doing something over and over again till it becomes a part of you, till it becomes a habit.

Our Routine

(1) Read your Bible
(2) Pray
(3) Be kind
(4) Be helpful
(5) Be thankful

Read: Joshua 1:8a (AMP): "This Book of the Law shall not depart from your mouth, but you shall read (and meditate on) it day and night …"

Memory verse: Dan 6:10b (NLT): "He prayed three times a day, just as he had always done, giving thanks to his God."

Life-Giver challenge: Start a journal entry of your Bible reading. For the next seven days, read your Bible, write the date, the verse or passage, and the version.

What I learned today:

_____

_____

_____

_____

_____

_____

_____

_____

_____

_____

What I plan to do:

_____

_____

_____

_____

_____

_____

_____

_____

_____

_____

LESSON THREE

Joshua 1:8 AMP

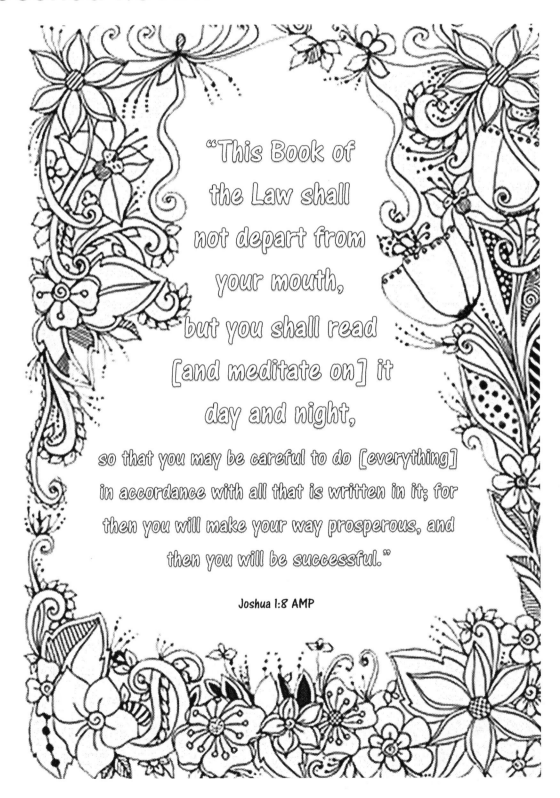

"This Book of the Law shall not depart from your mouth, but you shall read [and meditate on] it day and night, so that you may be careful to do [everything] in accordance with all that is written in it; for then you will make your way prosperous, and then you will be successful."

Joshua 1:8 AMP

Psalm 119:105 AMP

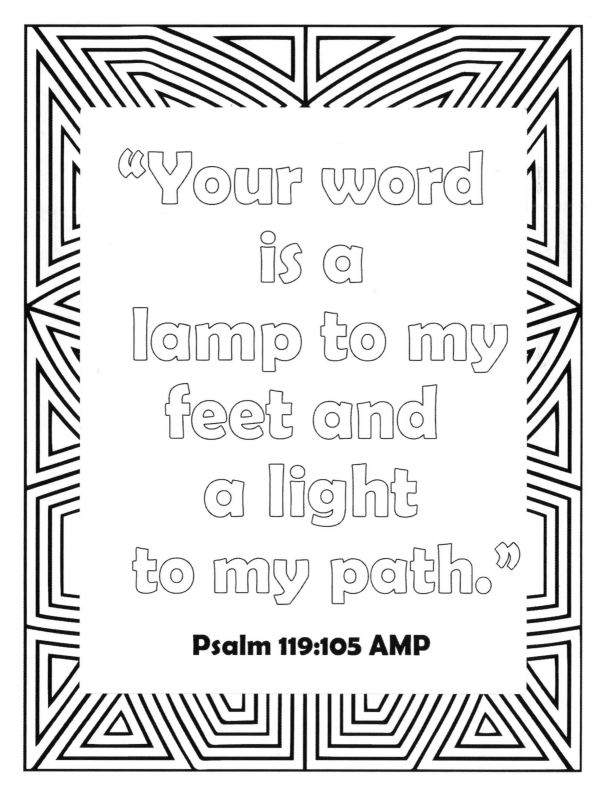

"Your word is a lamp to my feet and a light to my path."

Psalm 119:105 AMP

LESSON THREE

Read Your Bible

LESSON THREE

Maze 3 - Find your way out of the maze to your next activity.

Crossword Puzzle 3 - Read the Scriptures to help you solve the puzzle.

Scriptures – Joshua 1:8; Psalm 119:11; Ps 119:105

Across

1. God's word is a light to my _____.
3. Read this Book of the Law _____ and _____.
4. God's word is a _____ to my feet.
6. Do everything in this Book of the Law and you will be _____.
8. Read this Book of the Law _____ and _____.

Down

1. Do everything in this Book of the Law and you will make your way _____.
2. You shall _____ on this Book of the Law day and night.
5. This Book of the Law shall not depart from your _____.
7. I have stored God's word in my heart so that I may not _____ against him.

LESSON THREE

Read Your Bible
(ages 6-10)

Word List

1.Book   2.Word   3.Help   4.Make   5.One   6.Law   7.God   8.Night
9.Good   10.Kind   11.Read   12.Way   13.Thank   14.Day   15. Bible

---

```
D F R P L J N J H F C D V T W S
Q P L M J N B C F D R S X Z S T
Y H B G P K L B J U Z N J T I Y
X T X Y T I S D W H Y W S B N K
M N I Y O N E H V A B B N C W I
J E X R L D I B W T I U E A Z U
Q U D O M I P G O O D O Z Y I L
E L M N W V F O H V R B A L I Z
Y Q L Q K I E D P T H D N J E Q
A Y M O B U G T K H W M M Z P G
M Y O Z E X I I V A E Y B R H K
M B J A X U H W M N Y J D A U S
X A I D L D W L B K B R R I I L
V H K B F A T O A D Z J B V O S
S T H E L P U O P V E D Q K R T
U P Q G R E A D S S S O I L O G
```

Read Your Bible
(ages 10–14)

Word List

1. Apply 2. Depart 3. Thankful 4. Word 5. Pray 6. Routine 7. Book
8. Understand 9. Prosperous 10. Learn 11. Good 12. Read 13. Friend
14. Help 15. Family 16. Mouth 17. Success 18. Kind 19. Joshua 20. Law

---

```
D F R P L J N P J H F F C E D V
T W S Q P L M R J N B R N C F D
R S X Z S T Y O H Y B I G P L K
Q C N O S A I S L S T E Z E V B
K Z Z R I V F P P U S N E L K X
D M T I X K P E O L Z D X A Q J
Q C V Y W A N R B J O D L K Q P
H D D L R M O M O U T H R C Q
O R N P J C U U G S U C C E S S
K D E P A R T S B H E L P M Y J
H T H A N K F U L U R T K R W Q
J H U N D E R S T A N D L T V D
B T G R Z V L E A R N G O Y G Z
B O O K N H F A M I L Y J M L H
T W J X S G Z L K P R A Y K B M
V W I V F V S L I I N K W F G J
```

LESSON FOUR

Read Your Bible –
Understand, Apply, and Share
Student Review and Practice Sheet

What is Routine? Routine is doing something over and over again till it becomes a part of you, till it becomes a habit.

Our Routine

(1) Read your Bible
(2) Pray
(3) Be kind
(4) Be helpful
(5) Be thankful

Read: Matthew 13:1-9, 18-23 - The Parable of the Sower.

Memory verse: Dan 6:10b (NLT): "He prayed three times a day, just as he had always done, giving thanks to his God."

Life-Giver challenge: Continue journaling, include 1) What you read, 2) What you learned, and 3) What you will do next (how you will apply it in your own life and/or how you will share it with others)

What I learned today:

_____

_____

_____

_____

_____

_____

_____

_____

_____

What I plan to do:

_____

_____

_____

_____

_____

_____

_____

_____

_____

Matthew 13:23a NIV

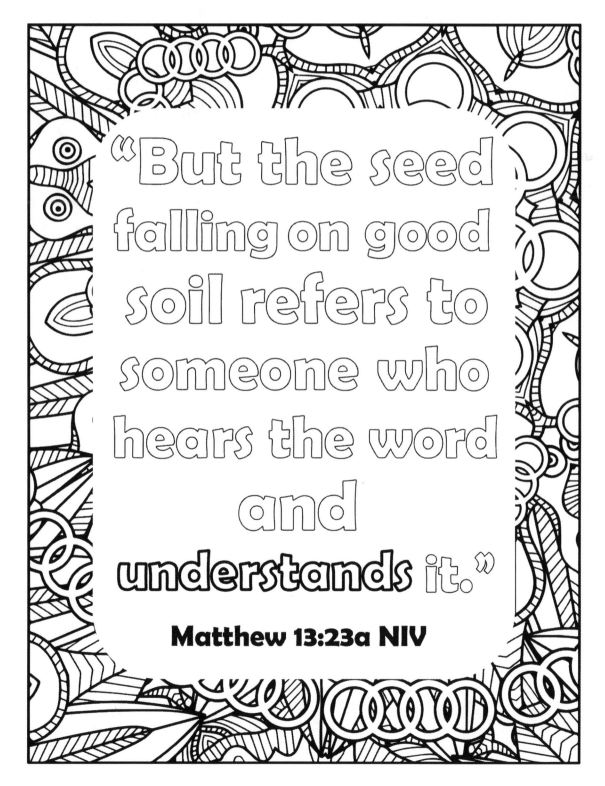

"But the seed falling on good soil refers to someone who hears the word and understands it."

Matthew 13:23a NIV

The Parable of the Sower

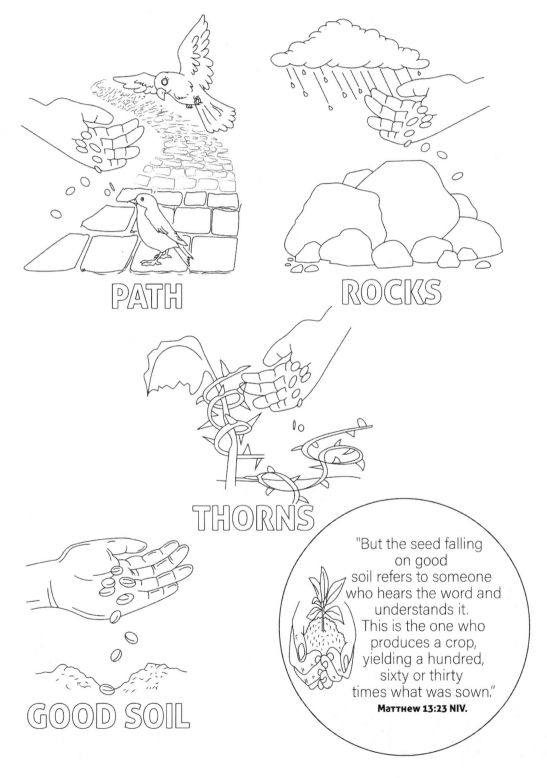

PATH

ROCKS

THORNS

GOOD SOIL

"But the seed falling on good soil refers to someone who hears the word and understands it. This is the one who produces a crop, yielding a hundred, sixty or thirty times what was sown."
Matthew 13:23 NIV.

Read your Bible,
Understand, Apply, Share

LESSON FOUR

Maze 4 - Find your way out of the maze to your next activity.

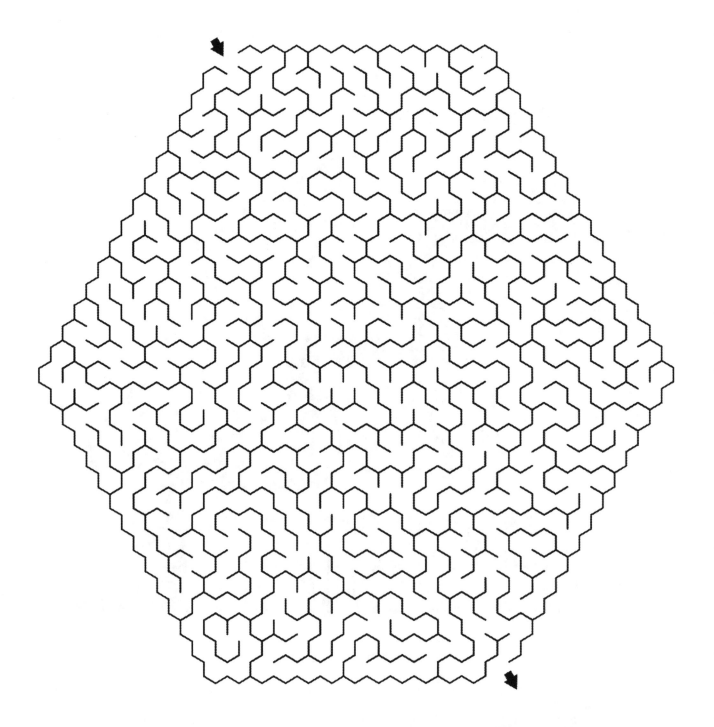

Crossword Puzzle 4 - Read the Scriptures to help you solve the puzzle.

Across

2. Some of the seeds fell on good _____.
3. Some of the seeds fell along the _____.
4. The seed that falls on good soil refers to the person who hears the message and _____ it.
8. The seed that falls on good soil produces a _____ a hundred, sixty, or thirty times more than what was sown.

Down

1. The seed represents the _____of the kingdom.
5. Some of the seeds fell on _____ places.
6. Some of the seeds fell among _____.
7. The farmer went out and sowed his _____.

LESSON FOUR

Read Your Bible: Understand, Apply, and Share (ages 6–10)

Word List

1.Read   2.Bible   3.Habit   4.Help   5.Apply   6.Share   7.Sow   8.Birds
9.Rocks   10.Path   11.Soil   12.Seed   13.Root   14.Life   15.Thorns

```
L P O R M W J H H R Z Z G P N H
J A O Y D Z G D C P S R P H E P
K T P R J G C N L D G D D N F W
R H J P T Y Z E H G W Z R S U J
H L Y V L H H C E C R H H S P A
N Z D D K Y A L U Q E U K K M T
Y T Q Z X T B L A R R C L S F R
H I V L C I I E A K O B E X L I
D S O W B L T H O R N S C A Z V
S A B Q C I S F Y E O W H Y P V
T M W C Z F R F S A F O C S U W
E Q U B S E E D W D D O T K S K
Z G H F O I X G S O W O U F H Q
O Q W M I X X I U S Z G E L L K
X Z D J L E D J M P V T W V Z O
X O P O C D E K G R C Y R Z A C
```

Read Your Bible: Understand, Apply, and Share (ages 10–14)

Word List

1.Read   2.Bible   3.Habit   4.Share   5.Apply   6.Understanding   7.Parable
8.Farmer   9.Soil   10.Seed   11.Path   12.Birds   13.Rocky   14.Shallow
15.Root   16.Thorns   17.Produce   18.Yield   19.Ground   20.Good

---

```
Z R N C J W O H J I F M P V U W
P T V A F G Y T B C L S R J R D
K Z B R D P K S L H N J E E G I
T S Q B X A D Q P Q R G M R R K
T T H U P R O D U C E R A G K W
Q B Z A I A P P L Y A F V N O D
Q I S B L B T M D F D M H R A Y
Z B H O Q L Z H L B O B T B K S
S L A W I E O S H Q Y K H C P K
B E R D M L D W O H D Y O C N U
A D E N G L U K Z J T R R D U H
P U N D E R S T A N D I N G F A
W V O I H I O C F Y E G S W G B
S K Y E F M S U N B I O T B O I
Y F B I H H E H N V V W R O O T
G R Z Z U V W O Q D T G U J D F
```

LESSON FIVE

Pray: The ACTS Method
Student Review and Practice Sheet

What is Routine? Routine is doing something over and over again till it becomes a part of you, till it becomes a habit.

Our Routine

    (1) Read your Bible
    (2) Pray
    (3) Be kind
    (4) Be helpful
    (5) Be thankful

Read: 1 Thessalonians 5:17, Philippians 4:6.

Memory verse: Dan 6:10b (NLT): "He prayed three times a day, just as he had always done, giving thanks to his God."

Life-Giver challenge: Pray using the ACTS method. Write in your journal, each time you use this method to pray.

What I learned today:

_____

_____

_____

_____

_____

_____

_____

_____

What I plan to do:

_____

_____

_____

_____

_____

_____

_____

_____

Philippians 4:6 NLT

Don't worry about anything;

Pray About

Everything.

Tell God what you need,

and thank him for all he

has done.

Philippians 4:6 NLT

1Timothy 2:1 NLT

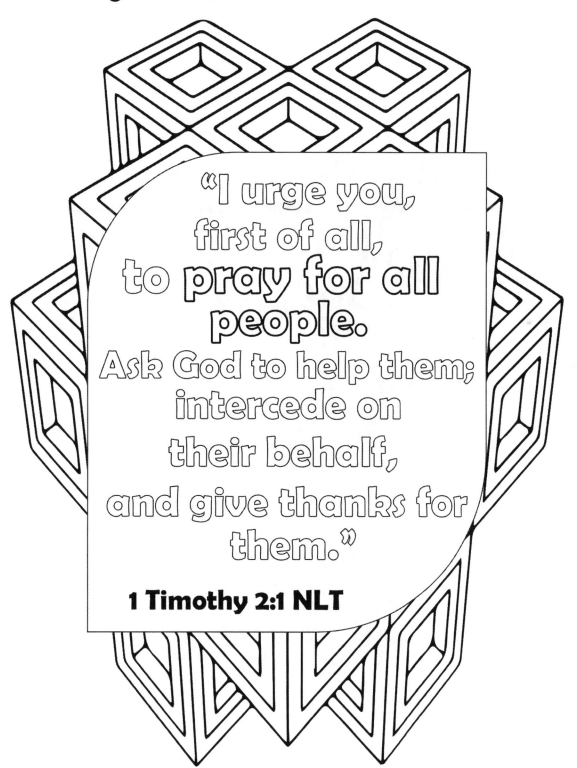

"I urge you, first of all, to pray for all people. Ask God to help them; intercede on their behalf, and give thanks for them."

1 Timothy 2:1 NLT

The ACTS Method of Prayer

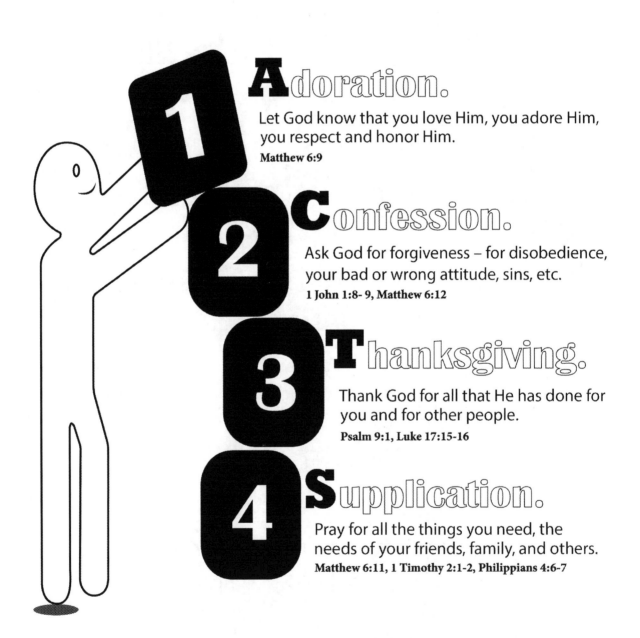

1 **A**doration.
Let God know that you love Him, you adore Him, you respect and honor Him.
Matthew 6:9

2 **C**onfession.
Ask God for forgiveness – for disobedience, your bad or wrong attitude, sins, etc.
1 John 1:8- 9, Matthew 6:12

3 **T**hanksgiving.
Thank God for all that He has done for you and for other people.
Psalm 9:1, Luke 17:15-16

4 **S**upplication.
Pray for all the things you need, the needs of your friends, family, and others.
Matthew 6:11, 1 Timothy 2:1-2, Philippians 4:6-7

Maze 5 - Find your way out of the maze to your next activity.

Crossword Puzzle 5 - Read the Scriptures to help you solve the puzzle.

Scriptures – Matthew 6:9, 1 John 1:8- 9, Matthew 6:12, Psalm 9:1, Luke 17:15-16 Matthew 6:11, Philippians 4:6-7

Across

2. When you pray, say our Father who is in heaven, _____ be your name.

6. Give thanks to God with all your _____.

7. Pray about _____.

8. Because God forgives our sins, we should forgive those who _____against us.

Down

1. We ask God for our daily_____.

3. Do not be anxious about _____.

4. If we _____ our sins, God will forgive us.

5. God is _____ .

Pray: The ACTS Method
(ages 6–10)

Word List

1.Pray   2.Three   3.Times   4.Always   5.Done   6.Habit
7.Thanks   8.Adore   9.Confess   10.Need   11.Friends   12.Family
13.Sins   14.God   15.Ask

```
A X B G X U Z N A W A B E T E Z
S Q W E Y Q C I V G T H N O X U
M K K J I E K C P I R T M J S D
L K E U Q P G N K V S L R N B R
C Z M Z G T O T I F A M I L Y V
Q O O G U H P P Z J R S W L C H
W I N T H A E G W A P I O P S S
B X J F E N T G T H R E E U J D
P N G J E K K V I A A Q Y N L L
W Z O U U S Q S M B Y S B E D I
X I H B A V S N E I T S G E O S
U P P R L D S D S T E H U D N N
X J P Y W P O C T S D H C S E M
B E M M A G V R I M K W C Y S Q
W G I W Y P N V E F U S S Y S F
I C J M S P N I O L F G I Z I C
```

Pray: The ACTS Method
(ages 10–14)

Word List

1.Pray 2.Three 3.Times 4.Always 5.Adoration 6.Confession
7.Thanksgiving 8.Supplication 9.Needs 10.Friends 11.Family
12.Forgiveness 13.Routine 14.Sins 15.God 16.Father
17.Habit 18.Ask 19.Everything 20.Request

```
G  E  T  C  C  C  X  J  A  D  K  G  S  W  P  B
A  D  O  R  A  T  I  O  N  H  I  C  U  P  L  Y
A  A  J  E  W  H  I  Q  W  S  G  O  D  Q  A  O
Q  H  N  V  B  A  T  I  S  U  S  N  T  H  L  D
R  O  U  T  I  N  E  N  Y  P  N  F  H  T  R  A
H  T  E  D  E  K  I  A  A  P  P  E  R  I  E  T
R  E  Q  U  E  S  T  T  X  L  R  S  E  F  O  S
D  V  M  J  R  G  T  C  O  I  A  S  E  D  B  G
F  E  P  M  X  I  D  Y  F  C  Y  I  M  X  S  C
Q  R  M  V  B  V  L  B  W  A  R  O  T  M  W  N
Q  Y  Z  A  J  I  C  I  W  T  T  N  I  V  C  D
O  T  H  H  M  N  Q  L  O  I  B  H  M  P  L  F
N  H  Y  A  O  G  A  S  K  O  R  D  E  W  V  H
Q  I  F  O  R  G  I  V  E  N  E  S  S  R  C  L
K  N  N  W  M  Z  N  E  L  P  R  D  X  T  K  U
P  G  F  F  R  I  E  N  D  S  G  N  P  X  J  V
```

LESSON SIX

Pray: The Five Finger Prayer Guide Student Review and Practice Sheet

What is Routine? Routine is doing something over and over again till it becomes a part of you, till it becomes a habit.

Our Routine

(1) Read your Bible
(2) Pray
(3) Be kind
(4) Be helpful
(5) Be thankful

Read: 1 Thessalonians 5:17

Memory verse: Dan 6:10b (NLT): "He prayed three times a day, just as he had always done, giving thanks to his God."

Life-Giver challenge: Using the Five Finger Prayer Guide, make a list of people you will be praying for this week.

What I learned today:

_____

_____

_____

_____

_____

_____

_____

_____

_____

What I plan to do:

_____

_____

_____

_____

_____

_____

_____

_____

_____

1 Thessalonians 5:17 NIV

"Pray Continually,"

1 Thessalonians 5:17 NIV

The Five Finger Prayer Guide

Pointer
People who point you in the right direction

Tallest
People in authority

Ring
People who are weak/helpless

Thumb
People who are closest to you

Pinky
you

The Five Finger Prayer Guide with examples. Version 1

The Five Finger Prayer Guide with examples. Version 2

LESSON SIX

Maze 6 - Find your way out of the maze to your next activity.

Crossword Puzzle 6 - Read the Scriptures to help you solve the puzzle.

Scriptures – 1Thessalonians 5:17, Philippians 4:6-7
*Refer to the Five Finger Prayer Guide

Across

3. The pinky reminds us to pray for _____.
5. The pointer reminds us to pray for people who point us in the right direction such as our _____.
7. When we pray, we have to also _____God.
8. The thumb reminds us to pray for people who are close to us such as our friends and _____.

Down

1. The tall finger reminds us to pray for those in authority for example the _____.
2. Pray _____.
4. Pray for all _____.
6. The ring finger reminds us to pray for those who are weak such as the _____.

Pray: The Five Finger Prayer Guide (ages 6–10)

X	M	Y	T	B	H	S	P	F	C	G	S	J	Y	P	L

Word List

1.Sick   2.Your   3.Learn   4.Close   5.Daniel   6.Tall   7.Read   8.Weak
9.Help   10.Pray   11.Five   12.Kind   13.Bible   14.Habit 15.Family

```
X M Y T B H S P F C G S J Y P L
S W C U G T W B D N P E D B A T
M Z Y E V C Y X Z X P N P H R H
N C H F I B N E Q X P O R O M E
C N F B J A L P Q X F W E A K U
J D I K I N D M F W V V I R A T
V K T K R B M D A N I E L U O Y
N K R A G L L K M F S I C K L L
B B E H L H P E I O C M R H D G
D L A B H L L S L S I W L L H C
V X D F E P X C Y Q D N Y J Y R
X K V H O B R O N B O G D I T G
M U S X A U O A Z A E Y G K B F
V O T E O B X E Y J K B W E H I
X J S Y V R I P M Q E I V B U Z
R T L P E Z J T S N U B G D J W
```

Pray: The Five Finger Prayer Guide (ages 10–14)

Word List

1.Understand   2.Teachers   3.Family   4.Continually   5.Finger   6.Three
7.Close   8.Kind   9.Leaders   10.People   11.Give   12.Read   13.Share
14.Bible   15.First   16.Weak   17.Routine   18.Pray   19.Thankful   20.Helpful

V	O	E	H	M	A	V	V	K	H	W	T	S	M	O	T
L	T	J	S	Y	P	U	T	I	V	B	R	H	Z	Q	U
N	O	S	X	B	G	F	I	N	G	E	R	X	R	R	N
B	U	K	H	L	C	B	R	D	H	B	I	B	L	E	D
R	V	P	R	A	Y	O	W	C	O	P	E	O	P	L	E
H	D	R	D	B	R	F	A	M	I	L	Y	K	R	S	R
S	B	T	G	I	V	E	A	B	A	M	E	R	O	L	S
Y	L	Y	T	B	T	H	A	N	K	F	U	L	U	Y	T
V	M	Y	A	H	G	Q	G	Y	Z	F	C	F	T	Y	A
M	S	M	W	L	V	R	N	W	Y	A	P	I	I	T	N
K	Z	X	K	T	F	X	U	W	V	L	Q	R	N	L	D
Q	T	C	T	D	L	E	A	D	E	R	S	S	E	C	V
U	B	V	C	Z	M	E	B	H	A	A	E	T	C	B	O
C	X	L	E	Q	I	I	F	N	T	B	K	A	K	D	W
C	O	N	T	I	N	U	A	L	L	Y	G	W	D	D	I
B	O	K	A	D	Z	Y	I	A	L	G	R	E	V	S	G

LESSON SEVEN

Review Lesson One to Six
Student Review and Practice Sheet

What is Routine? Routine is doing something over and over again till it becomes a part of you, till it becomes a habit.

Our Routine

    (1) Read your Bible
    (2) Pray
    (3) Be kind
    (4) Be helpful
    (5) Be thankful

Memory verse: Dan 6:10b (NLT): "He prayed three times a day, just as he had always done, giving thanks to his God."

Topic	What I learned
Introduction to Routine "But when Daniel learned that the law had been signed, he went home and knelt down as usual in his upstairs room, with its windows open toward Jerusalem. **He prayed three times a day, just as he had always done, giving thanks to his God**" (Daniel 6:10 NLT; bold added). *Do you have a routine? What is your routine?*	
Read Your Bible **"This Book of the Law shall not depart from your mouth, but you shall read [and meditate on] it day and night,** so that you may be careful to do [everything] in accordance with all that is written in it; for then you will make your way prosperous, and then you will be successful" (Joshua 1:8 AMP; bold added) *Do you read your Bible? What are the three things to ask God when you read your Bible?*	
Pray **"Pray continually …"** (1 Thessalonians 5:17 NIV; bold added). *Which method do you use – The ACTS method or the Five Finger Prayer guide?*	

LESSON EIGHT

Be Kind, Be Helpful
The Good Samaritan
Student Review and Practice Sheet

What is Routine? Routine is doing something over and over again till it becomes a part of you, till it becomes a habit.

Our Routine

(1) Read your bible
(2) Pray
(3) Be kind
(4) Be helpful
(5) Be thankful

Read: Luke 10:25-37–The Good Samaritan

Memory verse: Dan 6: 10b (NLT): "He prayed three times a day, just as he had always done, giving thanks to his God."

Life-Giver challenge: List 5 ways you will be helpful and kind this week.

What I learned today:

_____

_____

_____

_____

_____

_____

_____

_____

_____

_____

What I plan to do:

_____

_____

_____

_____

_____

_____

_____

_____

_____

_____

Luke 10:36-37 NKJV

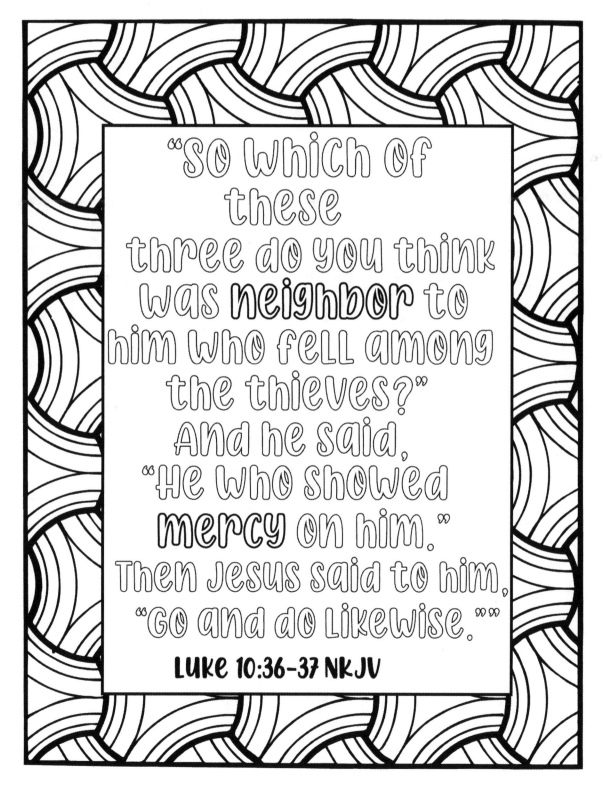

"So which of these three do you think was neighbor to him who fell among the thieves?" And he said, "He who showed mercy on him." Then Jesus said to him, "Go and do likewise.""

LUKE 10:36-37 NKJV

LESSON EIGHT

Be Helpful, Be Kind

The Good Samaritan. Version 1

The Good Samaritan. Version 2

Maze 7 - Find your way out of the maze to your next activity.

Crossword Puzzle 7 - Read the Scriptures to help you solve the puzzle.

Scriptures– Luke 10:25-37(The Good Samaritan)

Across

2. He took him to an inn and took _____of him.

5. The man was going from _____ to Jericho.

7. The _____ is the man who had mercy on him.

8. A _____who was going that same way, saw him and passed by.

Down

1. A _____ who was going that same way, also saw him and went away.

3. He bandaged his _____, used his own oil and wine to treat him.

4. A _____ came by, saw him and had mercy on him.

6. The lawyer asked Jesus what to do to inherit _____life.

Be Helpful, Be Kind
The Good Samaritan
(ages 6 –10)

Word List

1.Other   2.Pray   3.Care   4.Wine   5.Help   6.Bible   7.Read   8.Kind
9.Thieves   10.Levite 11.Share   12.Oil   13.Good   14.Each 15.Priest

```
C D B X C G J C C H X X Q Z L P
R W S C B S H A R E J I O S O X
E Q R Z G T L R U L Z X H T O W
C J F X O T H E R P D E Z E X A
V D Q V O H Z A V U N Z T N L N
Z Y Q R D I D D C I Q C E T V C
A P S V L E F O W N T Q S X I M
A E U U F V X N F D B E J C L P
F Z V B G E X R I N I A U J H Z
N N Z X W S C P D R B C R Z J I
L E Q P Z R N H P E L H G G F S
L K Z Q E D N J R A E K M G K Z
G F O N N A V L A D O A M T V T
B S O I D W A S Y G I G L M C Y
Z D K P L Z V F T Q J U E M L U
S E G S O F P L Z F N M N D R A
```

Be Helpful, Be Kind
The Good Samaritan
(ages 10–14)

Word List

1.Good   2.Care   3.Innkeeper   4.Steal   5.Priest   6.Neighbor   7.Samaritan
8.Pray   9.Read   10.Bible   11.Attack   12.Thieves   13.Ephesians
14.Wine   15.Luke   16.Wounds   17.Share   18.Oil   19. Levite 20.Routine

---

```
Y V Y R N V B Y X K D P Z K P A
C S M E P H E S I A N S A K U I
H J U P K Y W P R I E S T C J T
Y F F X E W N X M Y K Q T E X L
F I N N K E E P E R P R A Y A Z
L I G Q T R I L S H T P C N O L
W Y K D A C G U A B K Q K U F S
W F V C Z L H J M R J X O P Z P
Q M Q H Q R B L A P J L P Z Y G
B V H V W E O B R W O U N D S O
O F G Q L A R U I K L K K X L O
W J X B D D Q H T H I E V E S D
I L I N M I L C A I N Z V O I P
I B G G W Y P C N I N V N I W A
K S Y F B S W U W B S E F L T Y
R Q P I V N L Y O W Q S H A R E
```

LESSON NINE

Be Kind, Be Helpful
A 21st Century Good Samaritan
Student Review and Practice Sheet

What is Routine? Routine is doing something over and over again till it becomes a part of you, till it becomes a habit.

Our Routine

  (1) Read your Bible
  (2) Pray
  (3) Be kind
  (4) Be helpful
  (5) Be thankful

Read: Ephesians 4:32a

Memory verse: Dan 6:10b (NLT): "He prayed three times a day, just as he had always done, giving thanks to his God."

Life-Giver challenge: Look for a current day (21st century) Good Samaritan.

What I learned today:

_____

_____

_____

_____

_____

_____

_____

_____

_____

What I plan to do:

_____

_____

_____

_____

_____

_____

_____

_____

_____

Ephesians 4:32a AMP

Be Kind And Helpful To One Another, Tender-Hearted

Ephesians 4:32a AMP

Hebrews 13:16 NKJV

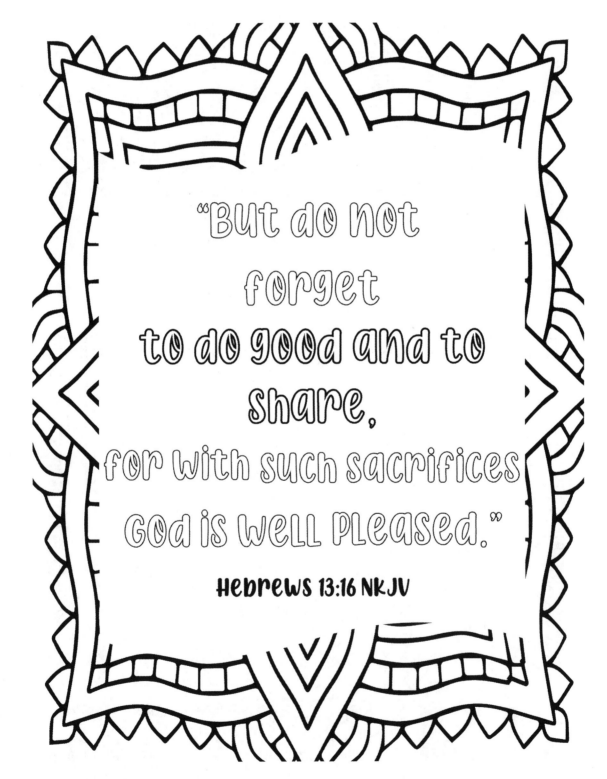

"But do not forget to do good and to share, for with such sacrifices God is well pleased."

Hebrews 13:16 NKJV

A 21st Century Good Samaritan

Maze 8 - Find your way out of the maze to your next activity.

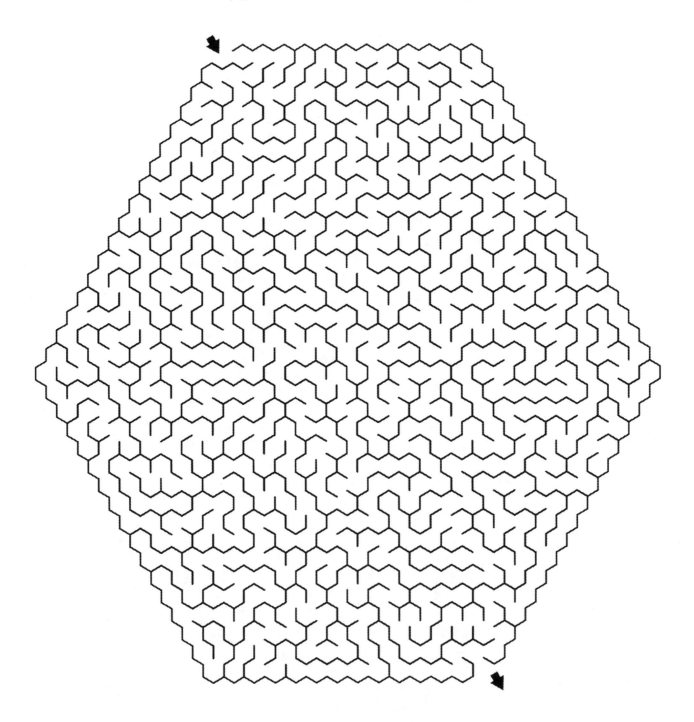

Crossword Puzzle 8 - Read the Scriptures to help you solve the puzzle.

Scriptures – 1Corinthians 13:4 (NIV), Ephesians 4:32 (AMP), Acts 20:35 (NKJV), Hebrews 13:16 (NKJV), Proverbs 19:17(NIV), Romans 12:13 (NLT).

Across

3. Always be eager to _____ hospitality.
4. Be kind and _____ to one another.
7. Do not forget to do good, and to share with those in _____.
8. Love is patient, love is _____.

Down

1. Forgive one another just as God in _____ has forgiven you.
2. It is more blessed to _____ than to receive.
5. Love does not boast and love is not _____.
6. Whoever is kind to the poor, _____ to God.

Be Kind, Be Helpful
Match the Verse Activity
[Look up the verse and match it].

BIBLE VERSES – Galatians 5:22-23(NLT). Proverbs 19:17(NIV). Galatians 6:10 (NIV). Acts 20:35 (NKJV). 1 Corinthians 13:4 (NIV). Ephesians 4:32 (AMP). Romans 12:13 (NLT). Hebrews 6:10 (NIV). Proverbs 3:27 (NLT). Hebrews 13:16 (NKJV).

1. "Love is patient, love is kind. It does not envy, it does not boast, it is not proud."

2. "Be kind *and* helpful to one another, tender-hearted [compassionate, understanding], forgiving one another [readily and freely], just as God in Christ also forgave you."

3. "Therefore, as we have opportunity, let us do good to all people, especially to those who belong to the family of believers."

4. "But the Holy Spirit produces this kind of fruit in our lives: love, joy, peace, patience, kindness, goodness, faithfulness, gentleness, and self-control. There is no law against these things!"

5. "I have shown you in every way, by laboring like this, that you must support the weak. And remember the words of the Lord Jesus, that He said, 'It is more blessed to give than to receive."

6. "And don't forget to do good and to share with those in need. These are the sacrifices that please God."

7. "Whoever is kind to the poor lends to the Lord, and he will reward them for what they have done."

8. "When God's people are in need, be ready to help them. Always be eager to practice hospitality."

9. "God is not unjust; he will not forget your work and the love you have shown him as you have helped his people and continue to help them."

10. "Do not withhold good from those who deserve it when it's in your power to help them."

Be Thankful –Ten Healed of Leprosy
Student Review and Practice

What is Routine? Routine is doing something over and over again till it becomes a part of you, till it becomes a habit.

Our Routine

(1) Read your Bible
(2) Pray
(3) Be kind
(4) Be helpful
(5) Be thankful

Read: Luke 17:11-19 (NLT) –Ten Healed of Leprosy, Colossians 3:15

Memorize: Dan 6:10b (NLT): "He prayed three times a day, just as he had always done, giving thanks to his God."

Life-Giver challenge: List five people who have helped you during this school year. Write a thank you note or make a thank you card for them.

What I learned today:

_____

_____

_____

_____

_____

_____

_____

_____

_____

_____

What I plan to do:

_____

_____

_____

_____

_____

_____

_____

_____

_____

_____

Colossians 3:15 NLT

...And Always Be Thankful.

Colossians 3:15 NLT

Ten Healed. Only One returns to say Thank You. Version 1

LESSON TEN

Ten Healed. Only One returns to say Thank You. Version 2

Maze 9 - Find your way out of the maze to your next activity.

Crossword Puzzle 9 - Read the Scriptures to help you solve the puzzle.

Scriptures – (Ten Healed of Leprosy) - Luke 17:11-19NLT

Across

2. One of the lepers came back to Jesus shouting _____ God.
4. Ten men with _____ were shouting for Jesus to have mercy on them.
6. Jesus told the leper who returned that his _____ had healed him, made him whole.
8. Only _____ returned to give God glory.

Down

1. As they went on their way, they were _____ of their leprosy.
3. Jesus told them to go and show themselves to the _____.
5. Jesus was traveling to Jerusalem, and he had reached the border between Galilee and _____.
7. Jesus asked the question – did I not heal _____ lepers.

Be Thankful –Ten Healed of Leprosy (ages 6–10)

Word List

1.Stand 2.Love 3.Kind 4.Pray 5.Jesus 6.Faith 7.Habit 8.Heal
9.Mercy 10.One 11.Glory 12.Lepers 13.Ten 14.Nine 15.Only

```
H  R  E  E  O  B  U  Q  U  H  N  K  Q  G  A  X
Q  D  G  U  L  D  Q  K  T  E  N  N  U  W  B  Y
G  Q  V  K  H  L  C  I  R  H  A  B  I  T  J  M
Z  Q  C  F  P  S  A  N  I  N  E  L  S  R  M  A
X  Q  Y  Q  C  F  R  D  N  R  R  A  T  E  S  S
O  W  P  F  Y  P  V  Z  T  U  U  U  L  U  A  L
O  V  B  C  F  O  Y  J  E  E  Z  W  U  F  U  O
A  S  T  U  X  K  R  S  N  C  F  T  B  R  B  D
W  D  V  B  G  Z  L  O  V  E  W  P  Q  Z  D  T
F  X  T  L  T  J  E  S  U  S  V  G  Z  B  B  A
X  Q  T  V  T  Y  P  V  T  I  D  X  X  F  D  S
Z  E  O  P  R  P  E  D  D  A  C  V  T  Q  M  V
I  U  A  O  G  L  R  B  B  V  N  D  Y  K  M  D
D  T  L  I  N  V  S  A  G  W  Z  D  T  B  M  O
G  G  Q  V  Y  L  Z  E  Y  D  A  H  Z  K  B  I
X  M  M  E  R  C  Y  V  D  I  P  A  T  B  L  A
```

Be Thankful –Ten Healed of Leprosy (ages 10–14)

Word List

1.Lepers   2.Samaria   3.Read   4.Nine   5.Heal   6.Habit   7.Routine
8.Thankful   9.Kind   10.Faith   11.Jesus   12.Priests   13.Always
14.Show   15.Pray   16.Glory   17.Master   18.Praise   19.Stand   20.Mercy

```
P N J N I P A L D Z E X B U G B
M R E A B X B F Z S S F R D G U
U Y I L J P O L D Y E H Z V I H
L I R E E C P N A N G P E O M S
G K E O S H A B I T I K U P J I
I W A F U T J N M Z P E R L Q O
X B D G S T S P A T T Q A E Q D
E K N C F H I F S E F E G P F B
E R P M A F T N T L H G L E Z D
Z W O Z K A H Q E R L P O R M Q
S A M A R I A S R Q O P R S T E
M F Y U T T N Z H B T R Y A L Y
M O K F L H K D U O O A I N Y R
M D I V N M F O W T W I N P R H
Z F K O F R U G X L J S O X C K
F L Z R C H L B A B M E R C Y R
```

LESSON ELEVEN

Be Thankful – Hannah's Prayer of Praise Student Review and Practice

What is Routine? Routine is doing something over and over again till it becomes a part of you, till it becomes a habit.

Our Routine

(1) Read your Bible
(2) Pray
(3) Be kind
(4) Be helpful
(5) Be thankful

Read: 1 Samuel 2:1-10 (Hannah's prayer of praise)

Memorize: Dan 6:10b (NLT): "He prayed three times a day, just as he had always done, giving thanks to his God."

Life-Giver challenge: Using Hannah's song as an example, write a poem or a letter to express your thankfulness/gratitude to God.

Show and Tell for the next time you meet. Bring your best take home activity sheet. You will present it to the class.

What I learned today:

_____

_____

_____

_____

_____

_____

_____

_____

_____

What I plan to do:

_____

_____

_____

_____

_____

_____

_____

_____

_____

_____

LESSON ELEVEN

Psalm 105:1 NLT

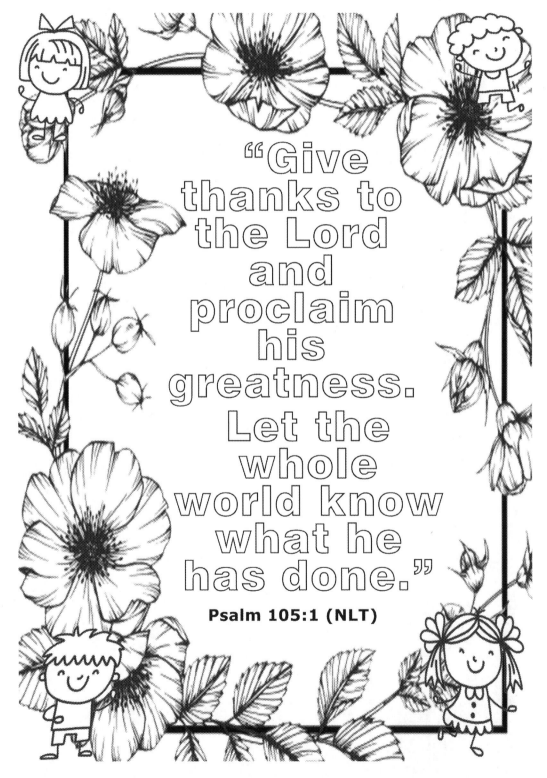

"Give thanks to the Lord and proclaim his greatness. Let the whole world know what he has done."

Psalm 105:1 (NLT)

Hannah's Prayer of Praise

"No one is holy like the Lord! There is no one besides you; there is no Rock like our God."

1 Samuel 2:2 (NLT)

"My heart rejoices in the Lord! The Lord has made me strong....."

1 Samuel 2:1 (NLT)

LESSON ELEVEN

Maze 10 - Find your way out of the maze to your next activity.

Crossword Puzzle 10 - Read the Scriptures to help you solve the puzzle.

Scriptures – 1 Sam 1:1-11, 1 Sam 2:1-10, Psalm 105:1

Across

2. Hannah made a _____ to God.
4. Give _____ to the Lord.
5. The priest was called _____.
6. Hannah got up, and went to _____.
7. Elkanah had two wives. One was called _____ and the other Peninnah.

Down

1. Hannah praised God and said there is no _____ like our God.
3. Peninnah had_____.
7. Hannah praised God for her son and said my _____ rejoices in the Lord.

Be Thankful
Match the Verse Activity
[Look up the verse and match it].

BIBLE VERSES - 1 Chronicles 16:8 (NKJV). Colossians 3:15 (NIV). Psalm 106:1 (NKJV). Thessalonians 5:18 (NLT). Ephesians 5:20 (AMP). Philippians 4:6-7 (NLT). Hebrews 13:15 (AMP). Hebrews 12:28-29 (NLT Colossians 4:2 (NIV). Psalm 100:4(AMP).

1. "Be thankful in all circumstances, for this is God's will for you who belong to Christ Jesus."
2. "Let the peace of Christ rule in your hearts, since as members of one body you were called to peace. And be thankful."
3. "Devote yourselves to prayer, being watchful and thankful."
4. "Don't worry about anything; instead, pray about everything. Tell God what you need and thank him for all he has done. Then you will experience God's peace, which exceeds anything we can understand. His peace will guard your hearts and minds as you live in Christ Jesus."
5. "Praise the Lord! Oh, give thanks to the Lord, for *He is* good! For His mercy *endures* forever."
6. "Through Him, therefore, let us at all times offer up to God a sacrifice of praise, which is the fruit of lips that thankfully acknowledge *and* confess *and* glorify His name."
7. "Oh, give thanks to the Lord! Call upon His name; Make known His deeds among the peoples!"
8. "Enter His gates with a song of thanksgiving and His courts with praise. Be thankful to Him, bless *and* praise His name."
9. "Since we are receiving a Kingdom that is unshakable, let us be thankful and please God by worshiping him with holy fear and awe. For our God is a devouring fire."
10. "...always giving thanks to God the Father for all things, in the name of our Lord Jesus Christ."

Which is your favorite verse? Why do you like this verse?

LESSON TWELVE

Grand Finale
Student Review and Practice

What is Routine? Routine is doing something over and over again till it becomes a part of you, till it becomes a habit.

Our Routine

(1) Read your Bible
(2) Pray
(3) Be kind
(4) Be helpful
(5) Be thankful

Memory verse: Dan 6:10b (NLT): "He prayed three times a day, just as he had always done, giving thanks to his God."

Topic	What I learned …
Introduction to Routine **"He prayed three times a day, just as he had always done, giving thanks to his God"** (Daniel 6:10 NLT; bold added) *Write out your daily routine.*	
Read Your Bible **"This Book of the Law shall not depart from your mouth, but you shall read [and meditate on] it day and night, …"** (Joshua 1:8 AMP; bold added) *Keep a journal of your Bible reading.*	
Pray **"Pray continually …"** (1 Thessalonians 5:17 NIV; bold added) *Using the Five Finger Prayer, make a list of people you will be praying for.*	

Be Helpful, and Be Kind **"Be kind and helpful to one another, tender-hearted …"** (Ephesians 4:32a AMP; bold added) *Find ways to be helpful and kind.*	
Be Thankful **"And always be thankful"** (Colossians 3:15 NLT; bold added) *At the end of each day, write down one thing you are thankful for.*	

Read your Bible, Pray, Be Helpful, Be Kind, Be Thankful

CERTIFICATE

OF PARTICIPATION

This award is presented to

_____

for Participation in

A ROUTINE FOR LIFE CURRICULUM

(DANIEL 6:10)

PRESENTED BY:

ON THIS DAY:

Read your Bible, Pray, Be Helpful, Be Kind, Be Thankful

ANSWER KEY

Lesson One

Word Puzzle (Ages 6-10)

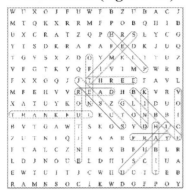

Word Puzzle (Ages 10-14)

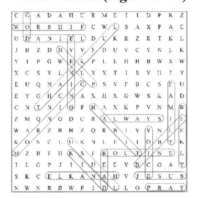

Crossword Puzzle

Maze

Lesson Two

Word Puzzle (Ages 6-10)

Word Puzzle (Ages 10-14)

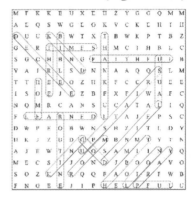

Crossword Puzzle

Maze

Lesson Three

Word Puzzle (Ages 6-10)

Word Puzzle (Ages 10-14)

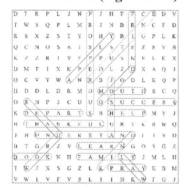

Crossword Puzzle

Maze

Lesson Four

Word Puzzle (Ages 6-10)

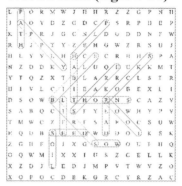

Word Puzzle (Ages 10-14)

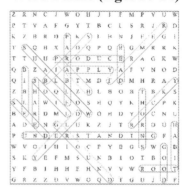

Crossword Puzzle

Maze

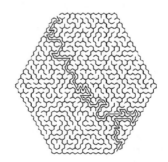

ANSWER KEY

Lesson Five

Word Puzzle (Ages 6-10)

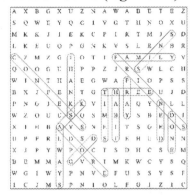

Word Puzzle (Ages 10-14)

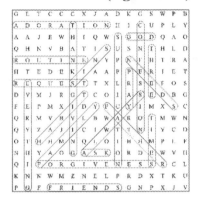

Crossword Puzzle

Maze

Lesson Six

Word Puzzle (Ages 6-10)

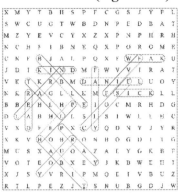

Word Puzzle (Ages 10-14)

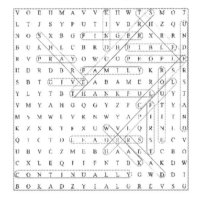

Crossword Puzzle

Maze

ANSWER KEY

Lesson Eight

Word Puzzle (Ages 6-10)

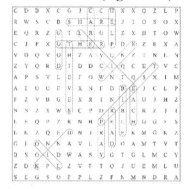

Word Puzzle (Ages 10-14)

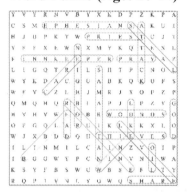

Crossword Puzzle

Maze

Lesson Nine

Crossword Puzzle

Maze

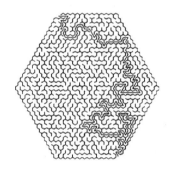

Match the Verse Activity

1) "Love is patient, love is kind. It does not envy, it does not boast, it is not proud." **1 Corinthians 13:4 (NIV)**

2) "Be kind *and* helpful to one another, tender-hearted [compassionate, understanding], forgiving one another [readily and freely], just as God in Christ also forgave you." **Ephesians 4:32 (AMP)**.

3) "Therefore, as we have opportunity, let us do good to all people, especially to those who belong to the family of believers." **Galatians 6:10 (NIV)**.

4) "But the Holy Spirit produces this kind of fruit in our lives: love, joy, peace, patience, kindness, goodness, faithfulness, gentleness, and self-control. There is no law against these things!" **Galatians 5:22-23(NLT)**.

5) "I have shown you in every way, by laboring like this, that you must support the weak. And remember the words of the Lord Jesus, that He said, 'It is more blessed to give than to receive.'"**Acts 20:35 (NKJV)**.

6) "And don't forget to do good and to share with those in need. These are the sacrifices that please God." **Hebrews 13:16 (NKJV)**.

7) ""Whoever is kind to the poor lends to the Lord, and he will reward them for what they have done." Proverbs 19:17**(NIV)**.

8) "When God's people are in need, be ready to help them. Always be eager to practice hospitality." **Romans 12:13 (NLT)**.

9) "God is not unjust; he will not forget your work and the love you have shown him as you have helped his people and continue to help them." **Hebrews 6:10 (NIV)**.

10) "Do not withhold good from those who deserve it when it's in your power to help them." **Proverbs 3:27 (NLT)**.

ANSWER KEY

Lesson Ten

Word Puzzle (Ages 6-10)

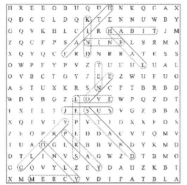

Word Puzzle (Ages 10-14)

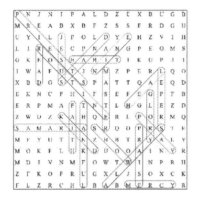

Crossword Puzzle

Maze

Lesson Eleven

Crossword Puzzle

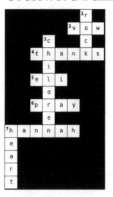

Maze

Match the Verse Activity

1) "Be thankful in all circumstances, for this is God's will for you who belong to Christ Jesus." **1 Thessalonians 5:18 (NLT).**
2) "Let the peace of Christ rule in your hearts, since as members of one body you were called to peace. And be thankful." **Colossians 3:15 (NIV).**
3) "Devote yourselves to prayer, being watchful and thankful." **Colossians 4:2 (NIV).**
4) "Don't worry about anything; instead, pray about everything. Tell God what you need and thank him for all he has done. Then you will experience God's peace, which exceeds anything we can understand. His peace will guard your hearts and minds as you live in Christ Jesus." **Philippians 4:6-7 (NLT).**
5) "Praise the Lord! Oh, give thanks to the Lord, for He is good! For His mercy endures forever." **Psalm 106:1 (NKJV).**
6) "Through Him, therefore, let us at all times offer up to God a sacrifice of praise, which is the fruit of lips that thankfully acknowledge and confess and glorify His name." **Hebrews 13:15 (AMP).**
7) "Oh, give thanks to the Lord! Call upon His name; Make known His deeds among the peoples!" **1 Chronicles 16:8 (NKJV).**
8) "Enter His gates with a song of thanksgiving and His courts with praise. Be thankful to Him, bless and praise His name." **Psalm 100:4 (AMP).**
9) "Since we are receiving a Kingdom that is unshakable, let us be thankful and please God by worshiping him with holy fear and awe. For our God is a devouring fire." **Hebrews 12:28-29 (NLT).**
10) "always giving thanks to God the Father for all things, in the name of our Lord Jesus Christ," **Ephesians 5:20 (AMP).**